GW00382249

Fall

Nigel Kent

First published 2023 by The Hedgehog Poetry Press

Published in the UK by
The Hedgehog Poetry Press
Coppack House, 5
Churchill Avenue
Clevedon
BS21 6QW

www.hedgehogpress.co.uk

ISBN: 978-1-916830-05-9

Copyright © Nigel Kent 2023

The right of Nigel Kent to be identified as the author of this work has
been asserted in accordance with the Copyright, Designs and Patents Act
1988.

All rights reserved. No part of this publication may be reproduced,
stored in or introduced into a retrieval system, or transmitted in any
form, or by any means (electronic, mechanical, photocopying, recording
or otherwise) without prior written permissions of the publisher. Any
person who does any unauthorised act in relation to this publication may
be liable for criminal prosecution and civil claims for damages,

9 8 7 6 5 4 3 2 1

A CIP Catalogue record for this book is available from the British Library.

for Kerry, Holly, Annie, Archie and Lyra

Contents

Part One: Falling

Part Two: Fallout

Part One

Falling

'Oh, how this spring of love resembleth,
The uncertain glory of an April day,
Which now shows all beauty of the Sun,
And by and by a cloud takes all away'

(The Two Gentlemen of Verona – Act 1, Scene 3)

October 2020...

They're cast as lovers,
and during their rehearsals,
she stumbles blindly
through the text, until he takes
her hand to give direction.

Riding the storm

October 15th*, Elle.*

This was a love
that had arrived
without warning,
lifting me off my feet,
knocking me off balance.
It pulled at me,
had brought down walls,
shredded what
we'd cherished,
and blown away the debris,
leaving my husband's hand
grabbing vainly
at the pieces
spiralling past.

But I learned
to lean into it, ride it,
for there was no lull:
it whistled for me,
all night long,
and shaped dreams
of a young couple
finding their way
across a wasteland
of upturned roots
under the moon's
benign smile
and a galaxy of stars
exploding silently
in a burnt-out sky.

February 2021

As soon as he leaves
she prepares for her husband's return,
bleaching bedsheets clean,
but she cannot wash away
the shame staining every day.

Confession

February 14ᵗʰ, Elle.

It only took one
touch from you to delete
all memories and plans.

You enlisted me as willing
conspirator in the plot
against my husband.

You made me a keeper of secrets,
encoder of words and looks,
adept in deception,

who had to endure chance meetings,
and casual conversations
like interrogations.

I jammed lines to family
turned my back on dear friends
as if they were informers,

and sought the safety of silence,
closed curtains,
and double-bolted doors.

All for a few smuggled hours,
locked together in borrowed beds
that never somehow feels enough.

He does not stop long;
yet she knows not to complain;
He grooms her to be
grateful for the rare titbits
he feeds her so sparingly.

A Matter of Form

April 5th, Jake.

I preferred a boutique hotel in Bath,
but she chose a cottage on the coast,
for the week her husband
went sailing with the lads.
It might have been postcard-perfect
in the summer months

but there was no spring sunshine,
no bright and sunny mornings,
for romantic strolls along the cliffs,
just an unrelenting sea fret
that wrapped itself around our eyes
and threatened us with the edge.

There was no entertainment:
no television, no signal for the phone,
just a chilly emptiness till bedtime
before a fire of sodden logs
that spat their disapproval
at our outstretched legs.

You wanted me to read
the books you'd brought
with lines that you had marked
but I preferred to watch you
whilst you composed a sonnet
extolling our relationship.

Your crease of concentration,
your sighs and suppressed moans,
your moist lips mouthing words
much too softly to be heard,
the urgency of your hand
tirelessly moving to completion,

which never came.

No matter how hard you tried,
you could not find the rhymes
that would not compromise the truth,
and a happy resolution for the volta
proved impossible to find.

July 2021...

They reject the script
and improvise their drama
with a cast of two.
To contrive a happy ending
they discard the husband's part.

Fall

July 20th, Elle.

Have you ever stood
on a cliff-edge,
feeling that primal urge
to lean into the void
and test the air
to see if it will
bear your weight,
hearing nothing
but the beating
inside your head,
feeling nothing
but the fluttering
in your chest,
thinking of nothing
but that first fledgling step,
until sense intervenes
and snaps you back?

Well, the day I left
him for you,
all that was solid
just slipped away,
into the chasm
beneath my giddy feet:
a vast, inviting emptiness
into which I stepped
with arms spread out
like wings.

September 2021...

He can't tell her yet:
honesty would wash away
her dreams and hopes.
Yet the sound of it leaking
keeps him awake at night.

Tripping the fantastic

September 9th, Elle.

I'd taken the postcard as a promise,
when he thrust it in my hand
the day I left my husband.

There were no words, just a picture
of two lovers on the beach,
dancing the tango under a storm-bruised sky.

They left no trail of footprints,
no trace of where the dance would lead,
as they zigzagged across the sand.

I folded the card, kept it in my purse
to sustain me on those desert days:
too many when he failed to phone

and proved himself more Northern Soul
that strictly ballroom, more at home
in baggy trousers than top hat and tails,

spinning, diving, dipping, solo,
always out of hold,
dancing to a beat he would not let me hear,

until the time that crease
became a tear beyond repair.

November 2021...

Left in the shadows
she fades and withers unseen,
longing for his
tender touch to restore her,
whilst the clock's hands sweep up time.

Picture Perfect?

November 15th, Elle

You said
I was the white space
that defined you,
that gave you shape;
that I was your life's
light and shade,
the one who gave you
the proportion and perspective
that you'd lacked.

So why did you leave me
screwed up in a ball
upon the floor?

December 2021...

She empties the box
where she kept his promises:
dead petals falling,
the debris of a summer
that was all too brief.

Shredded

December 18th, Elle

My hand
        hesitates
then feeds
the last of his letters into
        the lips
of the machine.

I watch
the pills of paper
join the heap in the bin
two-fists-deep.

Words that had kept me
        awake
        alone
in bed at night.

Words that had made
my heartbeat quicker
the mornings brighter
music sweeter
friends' jokes funnier
my laughter louder.

Words I'd come to crave and
        more.

When declarations no longer proved
        enough
I'd demanded stronger words:
        assurances
        promises.

Then stronger still:
        commitments,
        certainties

to slow my racing pulse
to ease lip-biting days
to shorten trembling nights.

Sedatives he could not supply
no matter how
        long and hard
        I'd pleaded.

Today rehab begins
though I can't prevent
my raw-rimmed eyes
        searching
the pile of estranged words
to find
        a marriage.

Part Two

Fallout

'Love sought is good, but given unsought is better'

(Twelfth Night – Act 3, Scene 1)

August 2020...

  Her husband floats,
  eyes fixed on a cloudless sky,
  untroubled by currents
  in a marriage of ten years
  that threaten to drag him under.

The end

August 12[h], Elle

I don't know when we
stopped
                    talking

when words packed up
moved on
like restless offspring.

Occasionally
they'd come back

duty visits   mainly
on birthdays, anniversaries
until the day neither
you nor I invited them.

Leaving
                    silence.

Of course we'd known
silence before

had relished once
the ellipsis of hands,
                of lips

when our conversation
continued all night

without words

but this silence was

                different.

This was the silence

after the slamming of a door

where there'd been
no door before

a door without a handle
without a key

the last full stop

    on the final page.

March 2021...

With her boho style
he barely recognises her -
a new wife he jokes -
but she had opened the door
on change, let a cold draft in.

Find the Lady

March 28th, Adam

You told me once
that when you were small
you loved to hide.

Always the same place:
in the cupboard beneath the stairs
under a crocheted blanket,
with the door ajar
to keep the demons
of the dark at bay.

Your mum would feign
panic and desperation,

Oh no! Where's Elle gone?
Where's my girl?
Elle! Elle!

Ignoring the giggles
and the wriggles
in the shadows,
she would let you
surprise her,
let you leap out
for a rapturous reunion.

Well, you're better
at hiding now:
camouflaging deception
with lies and smiles.

You're the dark
mistress of misdirection,
of the dexterous sleight of hand.

Now-I-see-you,
now-I-don't.

You're love's illusionist
who dazzles to deceive,
who turns lover into friend
guilt into innocence
suspicion into delusion -

Now-I-know-you,
Now-I-don't -

who leaves me
standing by the window
believing in the certainty
of a rapturous reunion.

May 2021...

Her betrayal cut
in two the love that made them one
but he tells himself,
most wounds will repair without
lasting signs of injury.

Playing with fire

May 15th, Adam

I lit the match
but didn't burn
your notebook
            today.

I know
            he's
in there somewhere,
            hidden
in the words.

I didn't
smoke him out
or commit him
to the flames

though some time
            tonight
you'll summon him
            again
to the room
that once
            we shared.

You'll conjure him
with images and symbols
to the rhythm of
your heart

an invitation
that he can't refuse
            to lie
between your sheets

where he will stay
till the final line
of your aubade

and dawn can't be
                    delayed
from carrying him away.

I lit the match
but did not burn
your notebooks today

for poems can be
                    rewritten
final lines
                    revised.

July 2021...

Fearing they're lost,
he reaches out for her hand
to retrace their steps
to try a new direction
but she is no longer there.

Ill-treatment

July 30th, Adam

You'd gone

by the time
I came back

to the echo
of a home

cleansed

of you.

Shelves cleared
drawers emptied
wardrobes stripped.

The waste of a marriage
dropped into bin bags
by the backdoor.

A purging:

the only treatment,
that would aid
recovery,
you'd insisted.

So tell me

why am I still suffering
from the discharge
of our past?

August 2021...

> She'd bagged and binned
> ten wasted years of marriage,
> dumped them at the door,
> so she could leave empty-handed;
> the past too heavy to bear.

Shadow-play

August 14th, Elle

When I moved out,
a shadow came with me:
it walks beside me
or just behind me,
a presence always
in the corner of my eye:
a persistent greyness
that drains the light
from the brightest day.
It pulls at my arm,
or tries to grab my hand,
won't be shaken off
or pushed away.

When darkness falls,
it follows me home,
creeping into my dreams
through the back door
where it taunts me
with a clock
projected on a screen
whose hands
spin backwards,
unwinding time
to that moment
which cannot
be undone,

when I fell
into another's arms
and guilt began
to stalk me.

September 2021...

When she walked away
she left him slumped in a hole,
a dark depression,
much too deep to climb out of,
too wide to be filled alone.

Feeling Down

September 12ᵗʰ, Adam

You let me

                                        DOWN

ran me

                                        DOWN

said I tied you

                                        DOWN

wouldn't back

                                        DOWN

wore me

                                        DOWN

turned life upside

                                        DOWN

shut hope

                                        DOWN

you might as well put me

                                        DOWN

I know it's a long way

                                        DOWN

I'm not looking

                                        DOWN

no I won't climb

                                        DOWN

and you *can't* talk me

                                        DOWN

no I won't calm

                                        DOWN

is this a

                break   DOWN

        a

                break   DOWN

        a

                break   DOWN?

December 2021...

He likes to lie in bed,
summoning morning dreams
to carry him to her
where life is as it used to be,
till work calls for his return.

Cold Water

December 21ˢᵗ, Adam

A jolt

as fierce
as the electric punch
of a defibrillator.

It IS you

not one of your imposters
who snag the eye
in busy streets
cafe windows,
supermarket queues.

We talk
tiptoeing
through the rubble
of our past

careful not to wake
recriminations
that roam its waste

and when provoked
bolt from shadows
snapping and snarling.

I dare to lead you

to where the future flows,
its currents strong and fast,
not suitable for those
who want to paddle
or tread water.

I leap in
inviting
you

to join me

but you decline.

It's far too deep,
too treacherous,
and anyway, you say,
you never liked swimming;
it's such a solitary pastime.

A year later...

He leafs through albums
of their wedding, holidays, parties:
the past lovingly preserved,
memories on which he drifts
into the future alone.

Love Letter #1

A year later, Adam

Yes, of course, there were others:

> a childhood sweetheart
> who turned dreams sour;
> a flirty uni girl
> who mistook me
> for Mr Darcy,
> a musician who wearied
> of my attempts
> to play the many variations
> of her tune.

but you were the one

> who saw clearly
> the reason for hesitance,
> for the absence of bouquets
> and boxes of chocolates,
>
> who stretched out your arms
> to catch me
> before I knew
> I was falling.
>
> The one who cleared away
> the clutter from the past
> so it couldn't trip us up,
>
> who sealed our future
> with certainty,
> leaving no questions unopened,

and who taught me
about home and family,
making 'you' and 'I'
into 'we' and 'us'

so that the ordinary
became extraordinary,
the imperfect perfect,
the broken whole again

with just one word,
one look, one smile, one kiss

once upon a time.

Thanks to:

Kerry, Holly, Annie, Robin, Tina, Mike, Wendy, Nick, Caroline, Stephen, Simon, John, Judy, Jane and Malcolm for their continuing interest in and support for my work.

The members of the Open University Poetry group for their encouragement and feedback.

Ellie, Kate, Jenny and Margaret for their kind comments.

Mark who continues to believe, much to my amazement, that my poems are worth publishing!